The Participative Leader

The Participative Leader

SUZANNE WILLIS ZOGLIO

Business Skills Express Series

IRWIN
Professional Publishing

MIRROR PRESS

**Burr Ridge, Illinois
New York, New York
Boston, Massachusetts**

IRWIN
Concerned About Our Environment

In recognition of the fact that our company is a large end-user of fragile yet replenishable resources, we at IRWIN can assure you that every effort is made to meet or exceed Environmental Protection Agency (EPA) recommendations and requirements for a "greener" workplace.

To preserve these natural assets, a number of environmental policies, both companywide and department-specific, have been implemented. From the use of 50% recycled paper in our textbooks to the printing of promotional materials with recycled stock and soy inks to our office paper recycling program, we are committed to reducing waste and replacing environmentally unsafe products with safer alternatives.

Mirror Press:	David R. Helmstadter
	Carla F. Tishler
Editor-in-chief:	Jeffrey A. Krames
Project editor:	Amy E. Lund
Production manager:	Jon Christopher
Interior designer:	Laurie Entringer
Art manager:	Kim Meriwether
Art studio:	Electra Graphics, Inc.
Compositor:	Alexander Graphics, Inc.
Typeface:	12/14 Criterion Book
Printer:	Malloy Lithographing, Inc.

Library of Congress Cataloging-in-Publication Data

Zoglio, Suzanne Willis
    The participative leader / Suzanne Willis Zoglio.
       p.   cm. — (Business skills express series)
    ISBN 0-7863-0252-6
     1. Leadership. 2. Executives. 3. Industrial Relations.
  I. Title. II. Series
  HD57.7.Z64   1994
  658.4'092—dc20   94–5494

Printed in the United States of America
1 2 3 4 5 6 7 8 9 0 ML 1 0 9 8 7 6 5 4

PREFACE

Upside-Down Organizations

It wasn't all that long ago that companies openly supported a philosophy of top-down management. Executives told middle managers what to do, middle managers told supervisors what to do, supervisors told employees what to do, and employees often told customers what they *couldn't* do. But fierce competition has changed all that. In quality organizations, top-down management has been replaced by push-down management in which decisions are made by those closest to the problem. The old organization chart has been turned upside down. Customers now drive the business, and managers focus on how to empower employees to continuously improve quality.

The Changing Role of Leaders

As leaders shift their focus to customers and quality, they realize that the old authoritarian leadership style does not work anymore. To achieve quality, service, and rapid response, leaders must utilize all available talent. They must find ways to inspire, involve, and empower employees. They must create a work environment that encourages commitment, innovation, and cooperation. Instead of evaluating, leaders now coach. Instead of doing, they delegate. Instead of telling, they facilitate. No one is expected to *boss* anyone. Everyone is expected to participate.

Benefits of Participative Leadership

While the shift to participative leadership may be a bit disconcerting at first, there are many benefits that make the change worthwhile for companies, employees, and supervisors. Companies obviously benefit from utilizing all available talent. When employee involvement is high, service, quality, and employee morale all improve. Employees benefit from participative leadership because they can apply more of their skills, influence workplace conditions, and continually develop new skills as they stretch for continuous improvement. Supervisors and managers benefit from the shift to participative leadership because involved employees perform better, get along better, and turn over less frequently. That means that supervisors have to do less prodding, checking, refereeing, and reprimanding. They can focus on more stimulating tasks such as planning, innovating, and facilitating teamwork.

Strategies for Success

As you work through this book, completing the activities and reflecting on your own work situation, you will learn how to:

- Inspire employee commitment to the job.
- Involve employees and enhance their motivation.
- Empower employees to perform at their best.
- Facilitate teamwork for a high-performance work group.

Embracing the Change

Shifting to a more participative leadership style will make you more valuable to your organization and more respected by those who report to you. Soon, you will take pride not in the doing but in the orchestrating. Your empowered work group will outperform most others and willingly set new challenges. Your influence will grow, and your contributions will be substantial. Embrace the change.

Suzanne Willis Zoglio

ABOUT THE AUTHOR

Suzanne Willis Zoglio, PhD, is an organizational psychologist who helps corporate clients manage change through planning, training, and team building. She facilitates planning and team meetings, coaches executives, consults on organizational improvement, and develops training programs for a wide variety of organizations. She is founder and sole proprietor of the Institute for Planning and Development, a management consulting firm in the Philadelphia area. Her clients include American Express, ITT Sheraton, Bell of Pennsylvania, Kellogg's, Hewlett-Packard, SmithKline Beecham, Bristol-Myers Squibb, Rohm and Haas, Quaker Chemical, Lockheed Missile and Space Co., HRB Systems, and the Federal Aviation Administration. Dr. Zoglio is also an active speaker and the author of *Teams at Work: 7 Keys to Success.*

ABOUT IRWIN PROFESSIONAL PUBLISHING

Irwin Professional Publishing is the nation's premier publisher of business books. As a Times Mirror company, we work closely with Times Mirror training organizations, including Zenger-Miller, Inc., Learning International, Inc., and Kaset International, to serve the training needs of business and industry.

About the Business Skills Express Series

This expanding series of authoritative, concise, and fast-paced books delivers high-quality training on key business topics at a remarkably affordable cost. The series will help managers, supervisors, and frontline personnel in organizations of all sizes and types hone their business skills while enhancing job performance and career satisfaction.

Business Skills Express books are ideal for employee seminars, independent self-study, on-the-job training, and classroom-based instruction. Express books are also convenient-to-use references at work.

CONTENTS

Self-Assessment

As a leader, you already involve employees to some extent. Before working through this book, assess how many participative behaviors you are currently using. This self-assessment will highlight areas you may wish to focus on as you work through these chapters. For each statement, check off the category that best describes you.

	Almost Always	Sometimes	Never
1. I believe that employee involvement is critical to my work group's success.	_____	_____	_____
2. I review our corporate mission statement with my work group regularly.	_____	_____	_____
3. I develop measurable goals with my work group.	_____	_____	_____
4. I communicate how my group contributes to the success of the whole organization.	_____	_____	_____
5. I establish clear performance measures with my group.	_____	_____	_____
6. I provide informal performance feedback to my group.	_____	_____	_____
7. I involve my group in determining recognition and rewards.	_____	_____	_____
8. I appropriately delegate responsibilities to my work group.	_____	_____	_____
9. I support my work group by providing the resources that they need.	_____	_____	_____
10. I emphasize the importance of teamwork.	_____	_____	_____

To determine your score, give yourself a 3 for each *Almost Always*, a 2 for each *Sometimes*, and a 1 for each *Never*.

26–30	You are already a participative leader.
20–25	You are well on your way to becoming a participative leader.
15–19	You have begun the shift to participative leadership.
Below 15	You are still leading in a traditional manner.

1 | Changes in the Workplace

This chapter will help you to:

- Understand typical changes in today's workplace.
- Identify how your workplace has changed.
- Recognize how workplace changes have influenced the role of leaders.
- Define what is meant by a "participative" leader.

Joe Simpson had been looking forward to his promotion for a long time. He'd been a solid performer for five years now and was even taking classes at night to enhance his skills. He felt good about becoming the new supervisor for B Group. He knew most of the workers in the unit and thought he could really make a difference.

Joe started planning for his new role by reviewing productivity numbers, checking attendance records, and asking about employee skills. All was going well until the day before he was to begin his new assignment, he came across a small book that his manager had given him. It was entitled *We're Not in Kansas Anymore: The Changing Role of Leaders.*

As Joe thumbed through the book, he noticed words like *empowerment, high involvement, participative, facilitative, collaborative, vision, commitment,* and *consensus.* He didn't see the word *boss* used anywhere. He read further. As he continued reading, he realized that the territory he was entering and the role he was assuming

1

were not familiar at all. In fact, he felt a bit like Dorothy in *The Wizard of Oz.* He muttered to himself, "You're right. We're not in Kansas anymore." ■

How Are You like Joe?

Perhaps you have felt like Joe at some time in your career. In fact, you may be feeling very much like Joe right now. Check off those statements below that apply to you.

☐   I am a new leader.

☐   Many of the leadership terms mentioned are new to me.

☐   I am quite comfortable with the term *boss.*

☐   I have no idea what makes a leader participative.

BEHIND THE SHIFT TO PARTICIPATION

Like many new leaders, you may be wondering why so many companies are shifting to a more participative leadership style. Unlike the days when a good supervisor was expected to rule with an iron fist, today's leaders are

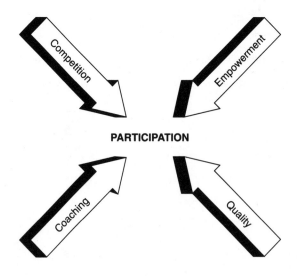

1

asked to be visionaries, coaches, and facilitators. But what do those words mean in terms of on-the-job behaviors? Faced with new expectations, many supervisors feel as though they are in alien territory. Understanding the changes that have made participative leadership necessary will make the territory more familiar. Changes in competition have necessitated changes in business goals that have created a need for new business rules and roles. Let's look at each of these changes.

The Playing Field Has Changed

Most companies today have to compete in an environment that is vastly different from the business environment of 10 years ago. While companies once had to outperform only two or three regional competitors to retain customers, they now have to be better than dozens of competitors. The playing field is slick, and it is filled with more obstacles. At every turn, a competitor is waiting to pick up the ball. Advances in technology allow customers to do business halfway around the world. Competition is global and fierce.

Surviving companies must deliver world-class quality to stay ahead. In addition, they must deliver their products or services faster than the competition. Because companies now compete globally, customers have more vendor choices, and they can demand better quality, better service, better value, and faster delivery. Perhaps your company has competitors today that you had never even heard of three years ago. Consider your own work situation.

Today's Challenges

Answer the following questions to determine how your organization's competition has changed.

1. What companies are considered strong competitors of your
   company?

   _____

   _____

   _____

1

2. Which of those companies were real threats to your business three years ago?

_____

_____

_____

3. What is your company's market share today compared with its market share three years ago?

_____

4. What would be the likely reason(s) if you were to lose a major customer?

_____

_____

_____

As you answered these questions, you may have broadened your understanding of how global competition has put customers in the driver's seat. To adapt, corporations are focusing on new priorities.

The Goals Have Changed

Business goals have taken on a new look. Companies that once focused exclusively on profit goals now set quality goals with equal enthusiasm. The axiom now is "Worry about quality; the profits will follow." Businesses that once set new sales goals have learned how fickle customers can be and how much it costs to attract new customers. These businesses now set customer satisfaction and customer retention goals. Organizations that once aspired to be better than their two or three competitors now focus on being the best in the world. Continuous improvement is not a fad; it is a way of doing business that is necessary for survival.

Setting New Goals

If you have been with your organization for more than a year, there is a good chance that you have witnessed a shift in company priorities. Describe how your company's goals have recently changed.

1. What new quality goals have been established?

_____

_____

_____

2. What customer service priorities have been established?

_____

_____

_____

3. What new emphasis is there on teamwork?

_____

_____

_____

As you described recent priorities for your company, you may have noticed that the goals are ambitious and would be difficult to accomplish under the old workplace rules. In many organizations, new goals have prompted new rules.

The Rules Have Changed

Quality and service goals cannot be achieved by a select group of executives. Such success requires the involvement of everyone in the organization to determine what customers want and how processes can be improved. Since employee involvement is so critical to success, companies have had to change some of their rules. Decisions and problem solving are no longer considered to be the exclusive territory of executives. Management is no longer expected to have all the answers. Instead, it is widely assumed that frontline employees are able to solve many operational problems more effectively than management. Problem solving is shifted to the level where there is the most expertise related to the problem. Decision making now involves those people most affected by the decision.

Few managers today would consider purchasing new equipment without extensive input from the equipment operators or starting a training program without assessing employee interest. Today, employees are asked

Traditional Hierarchy   **New Organizational Structure**

for input on topics that would have been considered out of their realm only a few years ago. They are also asked what customers value, how production can be streamlined, why a process isn't working, and how safety can be improved. Top-down decision making where management tells workers what to do is rapidly being replaced by push-down decision making where people closest to the problem decide what to do.

The rules of business today are different, because they support an organizational structure that is different. Traditional hierarchical structure is a triangle with management at the top, employees in the middle, and customers at the bottom. The old rules required managers to make decisions, employees to do what they were told, and customers to take whatever was offered.

Today, however, excellent companies have turned the organizational structure upside down. Customers are now at the top, driving the business. Employees are in the middle, listening to customers and becoming increasingly empowered to deliver what customers want. Management is at the bottom supporting the workers who are delivering the quality.

Are the Rules Changing?

Fierce competition forces companies to establish new goals and develop new corporate rules to increase the probability of achieving those goals. Identify any rules that have changed within your company.

1. In what ways is your company listening to customers more?

_____

_____

_____

2. What work issues are employees involved in today that only management would have discussed three years ago?

_____

_____

_____

The Roles Have Changed

For the new organizational structure to work, traditional roles must change. To ensure that customers are actually driving the business, companies make customers informal partners in developing new products, enhancing quality, and improving service. Focus groups, surveys, and advisory boards now involve customers. To increase employee commitment, leaders now tap all the talent available, asking employees for input on nearly everything. Frontline workers are involved in process improvement, cost containment, and innovation.

The roles of leaders have also changed. They are now expected to be coaches who communicate company priorities, facilitate teamwork, and support employees. Roles and responsibilities look quite different today.

Are the Roles Changing?

1. How have the responsibilities of frontline employees changed recently?

_____

_____

_____

2. Whose opinions are sought regarding most workplace changes?

_____

_____

_____

3. What are supervisors expected to do today that is different from what was expected a few years ago?

_____

_____

_____

As you described the role changes in your workplace, you may have noticed a shift toward more employee involvement and less authoritarian supervision. If so, your organization has begun to shift to a more participative leadership style.

THE MEANING OF PARTICIPATIVE LEADERSHIP

By now you have some understanding of how a participative leader is different from a more traditional, authoritarian leader. The chart below will help you understand on-the-job behavior of participative leaders.

Do's and Don'ts of Participative Leaders

Participative Leaders Do . . .	Participative Leaders Don't . . .
1. Communicate the big picture: company priorities, performance results, work units' connection to the large organization.	1. Withhold information and act as if the group is an island.
2. Involve employees in developing realistic goals, sensible performance measures, and appropriate rewards.	2. Tell employees what to do and hope performance is good.
3. Delegate appropriately and develop employees' talents.	3. Manage in a hands-on fashion.
4. Provide direction and resources.	4. Set people up for failure.
5. Facilitate teamwork with a focus on process.	5. Create competition and focus only on task.

Participative leaders are described as such because their job is to see that employees fully participate in decisions that affect their work. In short, participative leaders tap the full potential of their workforce. They orchestrate high performance by providing direction, information, and resources, and by facilitating group process.

In Chapter 2, we will discuss why this style of leadership works, and we will look at companies that attribute their success to increased employee involvement. In Chapter 3, we will examine why the shift to participative leadership can be uncomfortable for supervisors but also personally beneficial. Chapters 4 through 7 will describe success strategies for becoming a more participative leader.

1

Chapter 1 Checkpoints

✓ Today's competitive environment has brought about many changes in how companies conduct business.

✓ To compete, companies must be responsive to customers, innovative in product development, and fast in their delivery.

✓ To be responsive, innovative, and fast, companies need to tap the expertise of every employee, not just managers.

✓ To increase employee involvement, leaders must shift to a more participative style of leadership.

✓ Participative leaders provide information, direction, and resources. They also involve employees, empower employees, and facilitate teamwork.

2 | Success with Participation

This chapter will help you to:

- Understand why participative leadership works.
- Recognize how involvement has affected you.
- Identify corporate success stories.

Janice Sorenson is a risk management supervisor at a major insurance company in New England. She has been a supervisor for three years and has relatively few complaints about her job or her work group. Lately, however, she has become curious about a new style of leadership. Everybody seems to be talking about how to increase employee participation, how to empower people in their jobs, and how to create a high-involvement workplace. Janice wonders why this style leadership would lead to higher performance and whether any companies have reported success. ■

WHY PARTICIPATIVE LEADERSHIP WORKS

Like Janice, you are probably wondering about participative leadership. One question you might have is "Why does increasing employee participation work?" While there are many answers, three reasons stand out as particularly important. First, employee participation works because much of the day-to-day problem solving is transferred from executive offices to the front line where people have the most experience and information related to the problem. Second, employee participation increases motivation. Finally, high-involvement workplaces reduce organizational bureaucracy. A closer look at each of these factors explains why companies with high employee involvement outperform more authoritarian organizations.

The Right People Solve the Problems

As simple as it might seem, one of the reasons that participative leadership works is that the people who know the most about a problem are involved in solving it. Decisions are not the exclusive property of managers; they are the property of anyone who can contribute experience or knowledge. In this way, participative leaders make full use of all available talent. Those who are closest to a problem work on its solution.

Under more authoritarian leadership, even highly skilled employees might not be involved in decisions that affect their work. The following story illustrates this common, and often expensive, practice.

A utility company in Northern California was about to upgrade its heavy road equipment. The bids were narrowed to three by the time the vehicle operators were asked for their input. Although the highest bid proposal was not satisfactory to anyone, the vehicle operators considered the middle bid proposal the best buy, while managers favored the lowest bid proposal.

The company purchased the lowest-priced equipment. The managers' rationale was that although the middle bid equipment demonstrated a better continuous service record, its higher cost would not be offset by savings in repair costs. The managers also argued that the service contract offered by the lowest bidder seemed to be a very good value. What the managers did not consider (probably because they did not listen carefully to the operators) was that when a job is halted because of equipment failure, operators are paid while they stand around waiting for the equipment to be fixed. Also, such a delay often involves considerable overtime to meet a work order deadline.

2

After two years of numerous breakdowns and soaring overtime costs, the company's leadership decided to take the advice of the operators and purchase the better equipment. The earlier decision to buy the least expensive equipment was a costly mistake that would not have happened in a more participative work environment where the opinions of those closest to the problem would have been given full consideration. ■

Motivation Increases under Participative Leadership

Not only does employee involvement work because the right people are asked to solve problems, it also works because those people are *motivated* to solve those problems. By sharing information and involving employees in decisions that affect their work, leaders increase employee buy-in, or personal ownership. If you have ever been asked to work on a project that you believed was a waste of time or that you had no hand in creating, you can probably remember the level of motivation you felt: low or none. You may remember wondering whose bright idea it was to start the whole foolish project. You may also remember a different time when you were included from the very beginning. Perhaps you were asked if you thought the project was worth doing, who you thought would be good contributors to the project team, or what procedures would get the job done. You probably worked very hard to ensure that project's success.

■ How Has Involvement Motivated You?

To better understand how increased employee involvement affects motivation, consider recent work situations and how much you wanted each idea or project to succeed. First, describe three recent work projects: one that you were really excited about, one that you felt neutral about, and one that you really did not support.

2

1. A recent work project that I was/am excited about:

_____

_____

_____

2. A recent work project that I was/am neutral about:

_____

_____

_____

3. A recent work project that I did/do not support:

_____

_____

_____

For each question below, rate each of the projects you listed on a scale of 3 to 1.

3 = to a great extent   2 = moderately   1 = not much at all

1. To what extent did you influence early decisions on the project?
   Project #1:   3 ( )   2 ( )   1 ( )
   Project #2:   3 ( )   2 ( )   1 ( )
   Project #3:   3 ( )   2 ( )   1 ( )

2. To what extent was your experience or knowledge needed?
   Project #1:   3 ( )   2 ( )   1 ( )
   Project #2:   3 ( )   2 ( )   1 ( )
   Project #3:   3 ( )   2 ( )   1 ( )

3. To what extent were you listened to?
   Project #1:   3 ( )   2 ( )   1 ( )
   Project #2:   3 ( )   2 ( )   1 ( )
   Project #3:   3 ( )   2 ( )   1 ( )

4. Add up your involvement score for each project.
Project #1 Total: _____
Project #2 Total: _____
Project #3 Total: _____

Do you notice any pattern? If you are like most of us, the higher your involvement in the project, the more motivation you had. Check to see if your involvement score was highest for Project 1, which you were very excited about, and lowest for Project 3, which you didn't support. It is human nature to work harder at something when you have been involved from the beginning, when your expertise is needed, and when you are asked for input.

Participative Leadership Reduces Bureaucracy

Because participative leadership also reduces organizational bureaucracy, it empowers employees to do what needs to be done. Response time, flexibility, and creativity all increase. Nothing makes a work environment more sluggish than a rigid chain of command that requires employees to get approval for every minor action. Consider this example of a disabling bureaucracy.

Marie Elko, a customer service representative for an electronics manufacturing firm, was concerned that the six employees in her department were not helping one another as much as they could. Some people pitched in; others did not. Some co-workers shared time-saving techniques; others did not. The team seemed to have the potential to be much more effective.

So Marie read a book on how to develop better teams. Because she thought the book was just what the team needed, at her next department meeting she brought up the idea of reading and discussing it. With great enthusiasm, the team agreed to begin a team development effort the following week. Everyone would read one chapter a

2

week and meet at lunch to discuss how the material applied to their situation. They would rotate as discussion leaders.

Delighted with the enthusiastic response, Marie approached her manager about purchasing the books for the team. He responded, "Great idea. Put through a purchase order today and you should have approval in four to six weeks." Marie was crushed. The books cost only $19.95 each. The wait seemed so unreasonable.

Marie tried a few other avenues. She asked the company library and the training department if they could secure the books immediately, but the responses were the same. Marie went back to her team members to explain that they would not be able to get started for four to six weeks. Everyone was disappointed. Although the books eventually arrived, the spontaneous enthusiasm was dampened. The bureaucracy had diminished the team's effectiveness to improve its own processes. ∎

Under participative leadership, by contrast, innovation and responsiveness actually increase. When employees are empowered to make decisions that directly affect their work performance, they can solve problems and implement ideas spontaneously and see quick results from their efforts. Consider the policy of Nordstrom's department stores, an organization well known for its extraordinary customer service. Employees are encouraged to do whatever it takes to satisfy a customer. If that means delivering a forgotten credit card, buying a hungry customer lunch, or sending a gift tie because a suit alteration was not completed on time, that is what leadership wants. Employees are encouraged to be creative, and they don't have to wait six weeks or even six hours for approval. The system empowers responsible people to take responsible actions to meet organizational goals.

By limiting and, in some cases, eliminating the layers of authority that employees must penetrate in order to solve a problem, adapt to a challenge, or meet a customer's request, participative leadership increases the organization's ability to compete in a marketplace where quality and response time are prime determinants of success.

WHERE HAS PARTICIPATIVE LEADERSHIP WORKED?

Although you may now have a better sense of *why* employee involvement works, you may be interested in *where* it has worked. Consider the following examples of companies that have benefited from shifting to a more participative style of leadership and making employee involvement a top priority.

Large Companies Succeed with Participative Leadership

Large companies, such as Xerox Corporation, Procter & Gamble, and General Motors, all report 20 to 40 percent gains in productivity at plants that incorporate self-managed work teams . . . the highest level of employee involvement.[1]

Federal Express reduced customer service problems such as lost packages and billing mistakes by 13 percent in 1989 alone.[2]

Volvo, the Swedish automobile manufacturer, improved morale and reduced costs by 25 percent through the use of employee teams.[3]

Small Companies Succeed with Participative Leadership

Ralph Stayer, CEO of Johnsonville Foods, Inc., in Wisconsin, writes that by learning to tap the full resources of his employees he increased productivity, improved quality, and generated greater commitment from his employees.[4]

Doylestown Hospital, a 213-bed facility in Bucks County, Pennsylvania, introduced DIGs (Do It Groups) as part of its stepped-up employee

---

[1] J D Osburn et al., *Self-Directed Work Teams* (Homewood, Illinois: Business One Irwin, 1990).

[2] *Fortune*, May 1990.

[3] *Automotive News*, July 1989.

[4] *Harvard Business Review*, November–December 1990.

2

involvement effort in 1991. Participation in the DIGs was completely voluntary. The results were quite impressive. In just two years, hospital associates had completed 390 improvement projects focusing on topics as diverse as record confidentiality, patient falls, and pharmacy order turn-around time.

Rate Your Awareness

It is possible that relatives or friends have mentioned employee participation efforts in their workplaces. Or perhaps you have read that in some companies employees schedule their own work, select co-workers, and even meet with customers. Examples of employee involvement are everywhere.

1. What example of employee involvement have you heard of recently?

_____

_____

_____

2. How did the company benefit from the employee involvement?

_____

_____

_____

3. How did the employee(s) benefit?

_____

_____

_____

Expect More Participative Leadership

Other companies succeeding with teams and more participative leadership styles include American Express, ITT Sheraton, Rohm and Haas Company, Quaker Chemical North America, and SmithKline Beecham.

According to a national survey conducted by Development Dimensions International, the Association for Quality and Participation, and *Industry Week,* one-fourth of the organizations in North America have used self-directed work teams. Those companies include Xerox, IBM, Milliken & Co., General Electric, Corning, Digital Equipment Corporation, Best Foods, and TRW.[5]

Participative management works. It goes hand in hand with continuous quality improvement, enhanced customer service, and higher employee morale.

---

[5] R Wellins et al., *Empowered Teams* (San Francisco: Jossey-Bass, 1991).

Chapter 2 Checkpoints

✓ Participative leadership increases employee involvement.

✓ Three important reasons for the success of participative leadership are:

- Informed people make better decisions.
- Involved people are more motivated.
- Empowered people are more effective.

✓ Research indicates that high employee participation positively impacts quality, productivity, customer service, and employee morale.

3 | Managing the Shift to Participation

This chapter will help you to:

- Understand why change can throw you off balance.
- Describe the personal benefits of becoming more participative.
- Identify success strategies of participative leaders.

One Monday morning, the supervising engineers at a chemical processing plant met to discuss the recent transition to increased employee involvement. The supervisors had invited the plant manager, quality director, and training coordinator. First, the supervisors identified several tasks that the plant operators were now handling, and then everyone joined the discussion of how to help work teams come to consensus more effectively.

However, it soon became clear that the operators were doing better with the increased involvement than the supervisors were.

One by one, supervisors started complaining about how odd the new system seemed, how blurred the boundaries had become, and how no one was sure anymore of what it meant to be a supervisor. They seemed to understand why participative leadership was good for the company and good for the operators, but they were not so sure that it was good for supervisors. ■

CHANGE UPSETS THE BALANCE

Most supervisors experience some discomfort in the transition to a more participative leadership style. Like any major change, a shift in leadership style upsets the balance of things and causes some uneasiness. This uneasiness is often related to three factors: paradigms, power, and learning.

To embrace a participative philosophy, leaders must examine and often modify their paradigms (points of view or mindsets) about effective leadership. They must also confront any perceived loss of power, and they must learn new strategies for performing effectively. Let's look more closely at these three factors.

Old Beliefs Die Hard

Like most people, you probably hold some strong beliefs about how employees, supervisors, and managers should behave at work. That mental model or paradigm provides you with the rules under which you operate. For instance, if your mindset about people who report to you is that they are competent and hard working, you will likely delegate more to them than if your paradigm is that they are not very skilled or energetic.

On the other hand, if your paradigm of leadership says that leaders are strong personalities who seldom ask for advice, you are less likely to ask others for their input than someone whose leadership paradigm says that leaders are good listeners who fully use all resources available.

Leadership paradigms usually evolve over a period of time and are shaped in a number of ways. Your thoughts on leadership may have been influenced by the opinions of others, by articles in the business press, by actions of role models, and by your own experience.

Whatever the influences, your paradigm may define an effective supervisor as one who makes decisions, tells people what to do, and monitors productivity. Perhaps before you became a supervisor or manager, you even pictured yourself leading staff meetings, signing purchase orders, solving problems, and reprimanding subpar performers.

Now, it seems, the paradigm of effective leadership has shifted. In excellent companies, leaders are expected to listen more than lecture, to coach more than reprimand, and to facilitate problem solving more than fix things. Voicing strong opinions about the best way to accomplish something has been replaced with involving many people in creative problem solving. No longer is it considered a leadership asset to be on top of every detail.

Now leaders are expected to delegate more and focus on the big picture as employees handle day-to-day details. In addition, perks that used to come with the leadership territory, such as special parking places, private offices, and fancy dining areas, are rapidly disappearing. Such obvious boundaries are intentionally being blurred in an effort to create more joint ownership of corporate success.

While the rationale for this shift is well founded, the transition is not always easy. After all, you did not develop your beliefs about leadership overnight. They evolved gradually as you read, listened, observed, and even experimented. Eventually, they meshed into a paradigm that has probably served you rather well so far.

It is only natural that you would approach with caution any practices that seem to go against your rules. Your beliefs about leadership are familiar and comfortable; you are not likely to give them up easily. In fact, shifting a paradigm is a bit like breaking a habit. First, you must be aware of the habit, and then you must believe that the potential benefits outweigh the discomfort of the change.

3

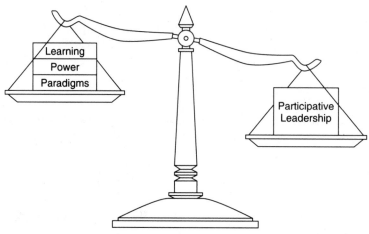

Change upsets the balance.

What Is Your Leadership Paradigm?

Recognizing your own leadership paradigm will help you to examine some of your underlying assumptions about what is appropriate behavior for supervisors and frontline employees.

1. How would you describe an ideal frontline employee?

_____

_____

_____

2. How would you describe an excellent supervisor or manager?

_____

_____

_____

3. Which work decisions do you think frontline employees should *not* be involved in? Why?

_____

_____

_____

4. Which of the above beliefs do not fit with a participative leadership model?

_____

_____

_____

5. Which idea(s) will be the most difficult for you to let go?

_____

_____

_____

3

Many Fear a Loss of Power

Another factor that causes some people discomfort is a perceived loss of power. Because some people equate control with power, they perceive a loss of power if monitoring tools (time cards, sales activity reports, materials request forms) are reduced in favor of more self-management.

These same people believe that by involving employees in important decisions, such as scheduling, hiring, and performance measurement, they are abdicating authority. Since information is power, many supervisors also fear they will lose power if they share important information (customer service ratings, productivity figures, safety reports) with employees who report to them.

While, at first glance, participative leaders may appear to be relinquishing power, they are actually enhancing personal power by increasing their influence. They create environments in which people want to work toward mutual success.

The key to dealing with any discomfort related to a perceived loss of power is to focus on the big picture—on what counts—rather than on outdated symbols, habits, or rituals. If you can mentally redefine power as the ability to influence others to join you in accomplishing worthwhile goals, you will be able to embrace participative leadership with less fear of diminished power.

3

■ Consider What Is Important to You

If you can identify which tasks and decisions are particularly important to you in your present job, you will be better prepared for sharing power when the opportunity arises. Answer the following questions based on your present job.

1. What tasks that you currently handle would be difficult to give up? Why?

   _____

   _____

   _____

2. What decisions that you now make would you resist sharing with employees? Why?

   _____

   _____

   _____

No One Likes Being a Novice

A third source of uneasiness associated with major job changes is the need for continued learning. Since most of us like to be recognized as competent workers, the learning curve required to master a new style of leadership feels awkward.

To learn a new style you must become a novice again, studying new techniques and experimenting with new methodology. Any status you may have achieved for being the best at what you do seems threatened. You may question whether you will be able to learn new techniques as fast or as well as others do. You may wonder if under the new system you will ever be able to perform as well as you have in the past.

All new learning brings with it a certain vulnerability. You have to admit what you don't know and risk making mistakes as you apply new skills. Therefore, you may be less confident of your ability to perform at the same level for which you have been recognized. However, as competition and technology continue to change at lightning speed, leaders no longer have the option of whether or not to continue learning; they must do so.

PERSONAL BENEFITS OF PARTICIPATIVE LEADERSHIP

Because change can be uncomfortable, it is important to focus on what potential benefits are associated with a change. Although you are probably now convinced of the wide range of *company* benefits associated with higher employee involvement, you may be wondering what, if any, *personal* benefits are associated with more participative leadership.

Since learning a different leadership style requires an investment of your time and effort, it makes sense to evaluate what you might gain from such an investment. You are likely to improve your job security, job satisfaction, and job success.

■ Evaluating Benefits

Check off which of the following benefits are important to you.

☐   Job security.
☐   Job satisfaction.
☐   Job success.

If you are like most of us, you checked off all three. Let's examine each one in more detail.

Job Security

Do you believe global competition is here to stay? Do you also believe companies that survive will excel in quality, service, and speed of delivery? If so, you may already understand how the security of your leadership position is linked to your ability to develop a more participative leadership style.

Research demonstrates that companies that tap the potential of their employees outpace and outperform their competition. Problems are solved more quickly, products are created and taken to market faster, service is innovative, and quality is outstanding. Employee turnover is low, and continuous learning and improvement are high. While there is no such thing as an absolutely secure position in a marketplace as turbulent as the present, jobs in high-involvement companies are generally more secure because organizational growth is more likely.

Even in companies that are downsizing, leaders who can adapt to rapid change are in the greatest demand. Both within their own companies and in the marketplace in general, participative leaders have greater marketability. Technical skills are no longer enough to secure a career in management. Leaders must be able to manage change, involve the best minds, facilitate improvement, and create an empowering environment. These are the people who can offer what quality-minded companies are looking for. In short, participative leaders will be in increasing demand, even as organizations reduce management tiers.

Job Satisfaction

While a secure job is important to most of us, job satisfaction is also important. After all, if you spend 40 to 60 hours a week at work, you are spending nearly half of your waking hours on the job. Wouldn't it be great if you could do less policing and more producing? Participative leaders have the opportunity to do just that.

As employees become increasingly responsible for more of the day-to-day decisions, such as scheduling, inventory control, safety measures, and process improvement, leaders can gradually do less checking up on people. With successful employee involvement efforts, employee accountability increases. Sensible measures are put into place, and results are measured against goals. There is less need for checking and an increased need for planning, coaching, and facilitating.

Participative leaders are able to focus on big-picture issues such as new product development, market niches, improved operational systems, and the development of corporate talent. Participative leaders enable, inspire, support, and guide. They develop a vision, a plan, support systems, and teamwork. They seldom actually execute a touchdown, but they create the environment in which the team wins on a consistent basis.

And More . . .

Supervisors and managers say that another difficult part of their job is dealing with disgruntled workers. The time and energy consumed in refereeing interpersonal conflict or managing subpar performance can be spent in much more satisfying ways. As employee participation increases, morale and productivity both increase, workers monitor more of their own performance, and groups resolve their own differences. Although your group may need some training in how to develop work-group rules or how to handle their differences, you will run interference much less frequently if you become more participative.

Once you assemble a good team of workers it is really satisfying to hang on to them for awhile. Participative leadership can add to your job satisfaction by reducing employee turnover. As a leader, you have an opportunity not only to help develop your people but to see the results of that development.

For most individuals the role of participative leader is challenging and satisfying. Although leading a high-involvement team presents challenges that are always inherent in any evolving system, the rewards can be very satisfying.

Job Success

Undoubtedly, as a leader, you are interested in achieving success on the job. You take pride in your work group's performance record and are well aware that any career advancement depends on the results you produce in

3

your current position. A participative leadership style increases the probability of your job success.

Research indicates that under participative leadership productivity increases, mistakes diminish, and innovative problem solving flourishes. When employees participate in decisions that affect their work, they become more committed, resourceful, and more motivated. This allows leaders to concentrate on success strategies such as measuring, planning, and connecting the work group to the larger organization.

As your work group's productivity increases, you become more visible to senior management and more valuable to your organization. Those are two benefits worth working for.

Success Strategies of Participative Leaders

How do you make the transition to participative leadership? What can you do to ensure that you are tapping the full potential of employees? The next four chapters describe success strategies that you can put to work immediately. You will learn how to inspire, involve, empower, and facilitate your work group.

Chapter 3 Checkpoints

✓ Shifting to a more participative leadership style requires moving out of your comfort zone.

✓ Changing your leadership style may be uncomfortable because:
- It is difficult to let go of strongly held beliefs.
- It is unsettling to share power.
- It is difficult to learn new skills.
- It is awkward to become a student again.

✓ When you become a more participative leader, you increase the probability of enhanced job security, job satisfaction, and job success.

4 | Inspiring Employee Commitment

This chapter will help you to:

- Understand why employee commitment is important.
- Identify factors that affect employee commitment.
- Learn steps you can take to inspire employee commitment.

It was the second meeting within a month that Albert Tomassi had called to discuss how his department might improve customer service. The first meeting had been a dismal failure as far as he was concerned. Several people came late, one person actually took a nap for a few minutes, and the rest of the group could be described as somewhere between unenthusiastic and totally uninterested.

Al did not want another meeting like that one. So he tried to determine what had been missing from the meeting. There had been no energy, little interest, not even any curiosity. In fact, no one seemed to care.

"That's it," Al thought. "No one cares about customer service. No wonder there's no commitment to improving it." Al's objective for the second meeting became clear: He had to make the department care. But would the effort be worth it? If people cared, would they behave any differently? ■

■ What Do You Think?

Describe what you think would change if Al were able to develop stronger commitment from his work group.

1. What positive employee behaviors might develop?

_____

_____

_____

_____

_____

2. What negative employee behaviors might decrease?

_____

_____

_____

_____

_____

You just described some of the benefits of inspiring commitment in a work group. How many of the following behaviors did you list?

BENEFITS OF EMPLOYEE COMMITMENT

When employees do not care about work priorities, their lack of interest is usually apparent. They show up late for meetings, withhold information, sit on any ideas, and generally demonstrate a lack of enthusiasm. People agree to complete assignments and then miss deadlines. Or they complete assignments, but not very well. You feel as though you are pulling teeth. Each effort on your part is met with blatant opposition or subtle resistance. It is clear that you and your employees are not on the same wavelength.

However, when employees are committed to their work, they behave quite differently. They show up for meetings on time, volunteer ideas, offer to help, and generally show enthusiasm. Assignments are not only completed on time, but completed in a quality fashion. People take pride in their work and want to be part of the team that is responsible for success. You can count on your group to work toward achievement of company goals. Little prodding is needed to get things done because people believe in what the company is trying to accomplish. Energy is high, and people work together toward the goal. Developing commitment within your work group takes time, but the results are worth the investment.

FACTORS RELATED TO HIGH COMMITMENT

To inspire commitment within your work group, you will need to consider these basic factors that affect the level of commitment in a work group. Generally, people demonstrate higher commitment to their work when they are proud of their company, confident of their company's direction, and clear about their connection to corporate success.

Pride in the Company

Some people take great pride in the purpose or mission of their company. They go to work every day primarily because their organizations are involved in saving lives, protecting the environment, promoting world peace, or increasing knowledge. Other employees take great pride in special accomplishments of their company. They like how it feels to work for an organization that rescues a child from a burning fire, develops a vaccine that will virtually wipe out a disease, or invents a computer chip that will make television interactive.

Still other employees take pride in working for a company that has achieved distinction in its industry. Perhaps the company is rated number one in its field for quality, size of market share, treatment of employees, or innovations. For whatever reason, when employees are proud of their company, they demonstrate more commitment on the job.

Confidence in Corporate Direction

Another factor that affects employee commitment is confidence in the company's strategic direction. No one wants to invest in a losing enterprise. We all want to put our energy into an effort that seems likely to succeed. If employees do not have a clear vision of corporate success or a clear understanding of the reasons for corporate initiatives, they will lose confidence in management's ability to position the company for success. Commitment increases when people are confident their company is on the right path to success.

Connection to Corporate Success

In addition to respecting the general purpose of the company and believing in the corporate direction, employees need to understand how their own work affects organizational success.

Many employees, however, do not recognize how their work affects the level of corporate success. An assembly line worker filling pill bottles may not understand that one error costs the company millions of dollars in recalls, or that increased production speed reduces consumer costs and secures market share. A data entry clerk in a bank may not understand that he enhances or diminishes his bank's reputation for service depending upon the accuracy of the statements he sends out. To be strongly committed to their work, employees need to understand how they fit into the larger organization.

THREE STEPS TO ENHANCED COMMITMENT

By consciously influencing the three factors that affect commitment—pride in the company, confidence in corporate direction, and connection to corporate success—you can inspire a new level of employee commitment in your work group.

Step 1: Develop Pride in Your Company

As a participative leader, you can develop pride in your company by reinforcing your company's purpose, announcing important accomplishments, and communicating your company's standing within your industry.

Reinforce Your Company's Purpose.   Regularly refer to your company's mission, post a mission statement and discuss department priorities in relation to your company's mission. If you do not have a formal mission statement, try developing one yourself by describing your company's purpose.

For instance, if you work in a hospital, your primary purpose may be to enhance health in the community. If you work in an accounting firm, it may be to ease financial burdens. If you work for a utility company, your purpose may be to provide energy.

Most companies have mission statements that are more complex than these, but you can begin developing a statement with a few important phrases that communicate the essence of why you are in business.

■ What Is Your Company's Mission?

1. In a sentence or two, describe the central purpose of your company. Explain, in the simplest terms, why your company exists.

   _____

   _____

   _____

4

2. What products or services are most important to achieving your company's purpose?

_____

_____

_____

3. What values does your company reinforce (innovation, integrity, cooperation, self-actualization) that shape your company's culture?

_____

_____

_____

Announce Corporate Accomplishments.   Focus attention on corporate accomplishments in many different ways. Distribute business press articles that favorably describe your company's achievements. Announce new customers that add prestige to your company's client list. Acquaint people with humanitarian projects that your firm is spearheading in the community. Invite senior management to talk about new products or recent successes. Hold joint meetings with other departments so employees can better understand the big picture. To assess and improve the attention you pay to corporate accomplishments, complete the next two activities.

Spreading Good News

Check any activities you currently use on a regular basis.

☐   Circulate articles about the company.

☐   Post new client lists.

☐   Discuss community projects the company supports.

☐   Invite senior management in to discuss recent accomplishments.

☐   Hold joint meetings with other departments.

■ What Else Can You Do?

List any other actions you can take that would enhance employee pride in your organization. Each action need not be a major event; you are trying to achieve a cumulative effect.

_____

_____

_____

_____

_____

4

Communicate Standing in the Industry.   Research various distinctions that your company holds and see to it that your work group is aware of each one. You can celebrate new distinctions, track regular rankings, and compare year-to-year ratings to show growth in industry position.

■ Using Corporate Rankings

1. Check any rankings that you can use to focus employee attention on the positive position your company holds within your industry.

   ☐   Customer service ratings.

   ☐   Number of products produced.

   ☐   Quality of products produced.

   ☐   Market share.

   ☐   Size of customer base.

   ☐   Number of employees.

   ☐   Profit margin.

   ☐   Number of new products developed.

2. Are there other rankings you could use?

   _____

   _____

   _____

Any of the rankings you checked should be communicated and celebrated on a regular basis.

Step 2: Develop Confidence in Corporate Direction

The second action participative leaders take to inspire higher employee commitment is to develop confidence in company direction. To do so, you should provide a clear vision of corporate success and good reasons for corporate initiatives. People have more confidence if they know where they are going and why.

Provide a Clear Vision of Success.   Nothing is quite so inspirational as a vivid picture of success. Just as a football coach works with his players to help them imagine their success in great detail—the sounds of the crowd, the rush of adrenaline, the feel of the ball tucked under the arm—participative leaders can increase the probability of employee commitment by providing an inspirational vision of corporate success.

Employees develop confidence in corporate success when they see a clear direction and believe everyone is heading in that same direction. Most companies communicate a vision of what they hope to be in three to five years, but you can emphasize the company's vision of success for a year, six months, or even a fiscal quarter.

Just be certain your work group knows where the company is headed. As Lewis Carroll wrote in *Alice's Adventures in Wonderland,* "If you don't know where you are going, you will probably end up somewhere else."

Clarifying Your Vision

Check off any idea that is appropriate for your work group.

☐   Invite senior management to describe the corporate vision.

☐   Relate work group goals to the corporate vision of success.

☐   Have work group members draw a symbolic picture of corporate success.

☐   Start each work group meeting with a reminder of the vision.

Provide a Rationale for Corporate Initiatives. Since most people are motivated to accomplish something when they believe there is good reason to do so, you can enhance employee confidence simply by explaining why particular corporate initiatives are necessary. It will help if you can describe any discrepancies between current and desired conditions when you are explaining the rationale.

For instance, in explaining that your company has made computer technology a top priority in order to increase product delivery time, you might also inform people that the last customer survey indicated delivery was only "satisfactory" instead of the targeted "excellent." Or when introducing a new corporate purchasing system, you could explain the annual savings that will result from use of the new system.

If there seems to be a good reason for corporate initiatives, employees will be more confident about the soundness of corporate direction. Problems arise when leaders *assume* that employees will understand the reason for a particular directive or *assume* that employees do not need to know the reason behind corporate decisions. Either assumption is dangerous and should be avoided.

Always communicate why corporate priorities are important. Are performance priorities clear in your work group?

■ Reasons for Performance Priorities

Describe below five corporate priorities. Then briefly describe the rationale for each priority. Finally, check off those priorities that you believe your employees feel are based on good reason.

Corporate Priorities	Rationale	Check
1. _____	_____	☐
2. _____	_____	☐
3. _____	_____	☐
4. _____	_____	☐
5. _____	_____	☐

Step 3: Clarify Your Group's Connection to the Larger Organization

To help your group see its relationship to the larger organization, examine why your work group is critical to corporate success, how your group affects the performance of other work groups, and how each member of your group contributes to your work unit's success.

Your Work Group and Corporate Success.   To examine why your group is important to the company's success, list your work group's primary products or services. Then, discuss the impact on the organization when those products or services are delivered well or poorly.

For instance, if you were the manager of an information systems department, one service your work group would provide is training on new computer software. If your group handled that task poorly there might be lost time, expensive errors, employee resistance to innovative programs, and even lost contracts due to incompatible systems.

The impact on the organization if your group handled the training well might be increased productivity, openness to technological changes, enhanced customer information, or even new customers.

Your Work Group and Success

After doing this activity yourself, try completing it with your entire work group.

1. List the primary products or services provided by your work group.

_____

_____

_____

_____

_____

_____

_____

2. Describe how good performance in your group supports corporate success.

_____

_____

_____

_____

_____

_____

_____

3. Describe how poor performance in your group blocks corporate success.

_____

_____

_____

_____

_____

_____

_____

If you can help members of your work group better understand how their collective performance can either positively or negatively affect organizational success, you will enhance employee commitment.

4

Your Group and Other Work Groups. Another way to emphasize the connection between your group and overall company success is to discuss the contribution that your group makes toward the successful performance of other work groups.

For instance, if you were the supervisor on the early shift of air traffic controllers at a major airport, you might discuss how your shift affects the level of performance of the afternoon shift. Obstacles to the next shift's success that could be created by your group might include failing to report faulty equipment, removing new protocol print instructions from a control station, or even failing to log unusual conditions in a particular air travel sector. Contributions to the success of the next shift might include sharing training ideas, volunteering to work on a different shift during the flu season, or agreeing to mentor new controllers.

Since such contributions to other work groups may not be obvious to people in your work unit, you can increase the feeling of connection to corporate success by discussing such contributions.

■ Your Group—and Others

It might be useful to complete this activity on your own, then ask other members of your work group to complete it with you.

1. List three work units whose success is affected by your work group.

    a. _____

    b. _____

    c. _____

2. For each group listed, describe three ways that your group helps that unit.

    a. _____

    _____

    _____

b. _____
_____
_____

c. _____
_____
_____

3. For each group listed, describe three ways that your group hinders that unit.

a. _____
_____
_____

b. _____
_____
_____

c. _____
_____
_____

To help your group feel ever more connected to overall corporate success, consider inviting representatives from other departments to your staff meetings to discuss what they need from your group in order to perform at their best.

Clarify How Important Each Member Is to Your Work Group.   Once you have clarified how your work group contributes to the success of the organization, it is important to emphasize how each of your employees contributes to the success of your own work group.

For instance, one of your team members may be creative, another may be logical, and still another may be knowledgeable. One member may contribute humor, another may contribute technical expertise, and yet another may contribute good meeting skills. Get to know your group members.

Your Group's Strengths

List each member of your work group followed by three strengths that person brings to your work team.

1. Name _____
   Strengths _____ _____ _____

2. Name _____
   Strengths _____ _____ _____

3. Name _____
   Strengths _____ _____ _____

4. Name _____
   Strengths _____ _____ _____

5. Name _____
   Strengths _____ _____ _____

6. Name _____
   Strengths _____ _____ _____

7. Name _____
   Strengths _____ _____ _____

8. Name _____
   Strengths _____ _____ _____

9. Name _____
   Strengths _____ _____ _____

10. Name _____
   Strengths _____ _____ _____

Chapter 4 Checkpoints

✓ Employee commitment influences the amount of interest and energy that employees demonstrate at work.

✓ Factors that influence the level of employee commitment are pride in company, confidence in corporate direction, and clarity of personal connection to overall success.

✓ Participative leaders encourage pride in their company by:
- Clarifying the corporate mission.
- Announcing company accomplishments.
- Identifying the company's standing within its industry.

✓ Employees' confidence in a company's direction is enhanced when leaders share a clear vision of success and a rationale for corporate priorities.

✓ Participative leaders clarify their employees' connection to organizational success by emphasizing how their work group affects corporate success and the success of other work units as well as how each employee contributes to the work group's success.

5 | Involve Employees to Motivate Them

This chapter will help you to: ─────────────

- Understand why employee motivation is important.
- Recognize factors that affect employee motivation.
- Increase motivation by increasing employee involvement.

It was noon, and the employee cafeteria was bustling with activity when Bob Cramer walked in. Employees at a corner table seemed to be particularly loud. As he walked toward the food line, Bob could overhear comments from the table.

"What's the point?" asked one employee. "They'll just turn around tomorrow and change their minds. There's no real reason for doing this."

"Yeah," said a second worker, "and the new production goals are totally unrealistic, anyway."

"Sure, look who sets the goals. Those guys haven't seen a shop floor in 10 years. They not only don't have a clue as to our capacity, they're too stubborn to ask us. Afraid we might actually teach them something about how to improve things around here."

As Bob continued past, he couldn't help wondering if any of his own people felt like those employees . . . left out . . . uninvolved. ∎

■ How Is Your Group's Involvement?

Like Bob, you are probably curious about how well you involve your employees. Rate yourself by circling **Y** or **N** in answer to the questions below.

Y N   **1.** Does your group know how the company is doing in relation to its goals?

Y N   **2.** Have you set achievable performance goals for your work group?

Y N   **3.** Has your entire work group gotten together to develop the best strategies for achieving your group's goals?

Y N   **4.** Have you and your group agreed on reasonable measures of success?

Y N   **5.** Do your employees have input into the rewards and recognition for your group?

Scoring: Give yourself 20 points for each Yes answer. Add up your points to see how well you involve employees. A score of 0 to 20 means you have hardly begun. A score of 40 to 60 means you are on your way to employee involvement, but you've definitely got a way to go. A score of 80 to 100 means your group probably feels quite involved; pat yourself on the back!

BENEFITS OF SELF-MOTIVATION

Most leaders would give anything to supervise a group of self-starters. For one thing, self-motivated workers require less work. They do what they are supposed to do so supervisors don't have to police them. They often do more problem solving than is expected so supervisors have to deal with fewer crises. They also change jobs less frequently so supervisors don't have to regularly break in new employees.

Self-motivated workers can be counted on to work hard and to make things work. Generally creative and energetic, they are more enjoyable to work with than workers with little motivation. Wouldn't you like to work with such a group? But where do you find them? Typically, you don't just *find* self-motivated workers, you develop an environment that creates them. You can do so by implementing strategies that positively affect key factors associated with employee motivation.

FACTORS RELATED TO SELF-MOTIVATION

Leaders can't actually motivate anyone to do anything. Motivation must come from within a person. However, leaders can influence factors that are associated with self-motivation. These are mutually developed goals, performance feedback, joint problem solving, and achievement rewards.

Mutually Developed Goals

Research indicates that employees achieve greater success when they participate in the development of performance goals. Ideally, workplace goals should be developed by the people charged with achieving them. Minimally, workers need to have input regarding the clarity and attainability of goals. You will see little energy expended on goals that employees believe are unimportant, unrealistic, or both.

Has anyone ever set goals for you with little or no consideration for your ideas? Perhaps you were told to increase business by $500,000 annually or to reduce costs by $50,000 in six months, or to expand your services to include 24-hour delivery.

Salespeople deal with this problem all the time. Someone decides that $4 million in new sales per region would be terrific. The regions receive an edict, and regardless of how unattainable employees believe the target to be, the $4 million figure is posted. In such cases, leaders will often wonder why the team does not seem motivated. The reason: The employees were not involved.

Feedback on Performance

A second factor associated with self-motivation is performance feedback, or information on the results of work efforts. If leaders want a more energetic workforce, they must let employees know how they are doing or establish systems that will allow employees to measure results themselves.

Performance feedback motivates employees because it indicates whether they should continue the same behavior or make adjustments. One theory of motivation, called discrepancy theory, explains why feedback is motivating. If a person is made aware of a gap between the results achieved (for example, poor ratings on courtesy) and the desired condition (for example, customer satisfaction), the person will be motivated to reduce the gap.

Besides being motivating, performance feedback is *directing;* it shows people how to change. To further understand this principle, try this experiment. Give a blindfolded individual a crumpled-up piece of paper. Set a wastebasket 10 to 12 feet away and ask the person to toss the paper into the basket. Chances are the person will miss. Ask the person to try again, but this time provide feedback on the first attempt ("you were a little off to the right"). If the person doesn't make the basket on the second try, provide more specific feedback ("that time you were a little short, but you centered it well").

The person will probably make the basket within three or four tries if assisted by feedback. Without feedback on performance results, the person may give up. Without feedback, employee motivation is low.

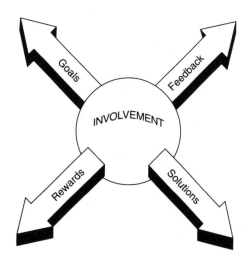

Joint Problem Solving

A person's enthusiasm for a particular course of action increases if she had a hand in determining the best course of action. Ownership for an idea or a process is highly dependent upon involvement.

To understand this factor better, consider a time when you were not achieving the results you wanted and someone in authority told you to do it differently. There was no collaborative brainstorming or meaningful discussion of cause and analysis; you were just told to do something differently. Do you remember being very motivated to take the new course of action? Probably not. Perhaps you can even remember how you felt as a child whenever someone strongly suggested that you change course and do things a better way. Did you resist the advice, perhaps even resent the intrusion? Probably.

Suppose you were told to conduct a department meeting on techniques for lifting heavy objects. What would your response be to such a directive? If you are like most leaders, you would wonder, "What in the world for?" Suppose upon asking that logical question, you were told, "Got me. Somebody upstairs wants it done." How motivated would you be to conduct the meeting? Probably not very motivated. In fact, you might decide not to call a meeting at all to test the directive and see if anyone pushed the issue. Or you might decide to go through the motions of a meeting by assembling your group, distributing an instruction sheet, and considering your obligation fulfilled.

However, suppose instead of a directive you were given data that showed back injuries in your area this quarter far exceeded the company's average, and you were asked to fix the problem. Would you be motivated to conduct training? Or suppose you were told that the company could lower its insurance premium by $300,000 next year if safety meetings were held, and you were asked if such meetings were feasible. Would you be motivated to conduct the meetings? Probably, because you would understand the need for the meetings and you would be involved in the details.

Most of us do not like being told how to fix something we feel responsible for. Employees are more motivated when they are involved in deciding which course of action is best.

Achievement Rewards

The fourth key factor associated with employee motivation is the probability of meaningful rewards. The expectancy theory of motivation explains that people are motivated to succeed if they expect they *will* succeed and that such success will result in rewards that they value.

This does not mean that rewards must be monetary or even leader driven. Employees may find the challenge of a task or the recognition of peers rewarding. However, they must benefit in some way for working hard.

FOUR STEPS TO INCREASING MOTIVATION

You can enhance motivation in your work group by influencing the four factors we've just discussed: mutually developed goals, performance feedback, joint problem solving, and achievement rewards. Let's examine specific actions you can take as a participative leader to increase employee involvement in each of these areas.

Step 1: Agree on Attainable Goals

Two elements are important if goals are to enhance employee motivation: The goals must be mutually developed, and they must be attainable. If either of these elements is missing, motivation will be lessened.

Develop Performance Goals with Your Work Group. While many traditional leaders believe they must set performance goals themselves, participative leaders understand the power of involving employees in establishing work group targets. When employees provide input on work goals, they are basically writing their own performance contracts. They are agreeing to deliver certain results.

When employees help determine performance challenges, they feel more in control, and control is an important element in human motivation. As adults, most of us want to determine our own destiny. We want to direct our own future and have a say in how hard we work and how our energy will be used.

Ironically, employees who help establish performance goals often develop more challenging goals than their leaders would impose.

■ Involve Employees in Goal Setting

Check off the involvement techniques that would work in your group.

☐   Ask each worker to write three goals to bring to a team meeting.

☐   Post six performance goals at your next meeting and ask employees to individually rank them in terms of importance to the company.

☐   Distribute major organizational goals and ask each worker to establish one personal performance goal for each organizational goal.

☐   Discuss significant performance data (production numbers, service ratings, department costs); identify three improvement priorities; assign one improvement priority to each of three groups of employees; and ask each group to develop specific goals for their assigned improvement area.

Make Sure Goals Are Reasonable.   Because employees frequently set ambitious goals, leaders may need to help employees focus on attainable goals. That does not mean you should squelch enthusiasm for new challenges, but it does mean you should play a role in assessing the probability of success. You can do that by calling attention to past success levels, reminding people of any changes in resources (reduction in staff or budget), and discussing any conditions necessary for group success.

A primary task for participative leaders is to assist employees in creating challenging goals that they have a good chance of achieving.

Rate Your Group's Goals

List three to five priority goals for your work group and then rate each goal 3, 2, or 1, according to how attainable and challenging it is.

3 = very   2 = somewhat   1 = not very

Goals	How challenging?			How attainable?		
1. _____	( )3	( )2	( )1	( )3	( )2	( )1
2. _____	( )3	( )2	( )1	( )3	( )2	( )1
3. _____	( )3	( )2	( )1	( )3	( )2	( )1
4. _____	( )3	( )2	( )1	( )3	( )2	( )1
5. _____	( )3	( )2	( )1	( )3	( )2	( )1

Step 2: Provide Performance Feedback

A saying that is often heard in quality-conscious organizations is "What gets measured gets done." The truth of this statement lies in the fact that feedback is motivating and motivated employees get things done. Participative leaders make sure that employees know how well they are performing against relevant measures. Leaders can also provide informal feedback that lets employees know that they are appreciated.

Measure and Communicate Performance Results. To understand why performance feedback is so important to motivation, consider how you felt on the day that a teacher was to post exam results or on the day of your latest performance appraisal. Even playing a computer game will demonstrate the principle. Why do you suppose that game designers make sure your successes or failures are flashed immediately on the screen? Because performance feedback is motivating.

For sustained motivation, feedback should be regular, specific, and related to work group goals. In many organizations, employees receive a vague evaluation once a year but little specific feedback on the results of their work efforts.

Very often the reason that employees do not receive performance feedback is that performance is not measured. Participative leaders make sure that important performance areas are measured. If a goal is important to department or company success, it should be measured, and the results should be communicated to employees.

█ **M e a s u r i n g   R e s u l t s**

List your group's priority performance goals and how each is currently being measured. Circle **Y** if the results are discussed.

Goals	Measures	Results Discussed?
_____	_____	Y N
_____	_____	Y N
_____	_____	Y N
_____	_____	Y N

Let Employees Know That You Appreciate Them.   You can provide informal positive feedback to your work group by speaking well of its progress, recognizing group accomplishments, being available when employees need you, and making issues that are important to your employees important to you. You can also provide positive feedback by speaking well of your department outside of your work area (word always gets back to employees). Consider your spontaneous comments, management reports on your group, or presentations of your employees' opinions at management meetings.

Informal Feedback—How Much?

1. Check off any actions that your employees would say you take regularly.

   ☐   I regularly speak well of my employees.

   ☐   I recognize accomplishments of my work group.

   ☐   I am available when my group needs me.

   ☐   I give top priority to issues that are important to my group.

   ☐   I keep management informed of my group's accomplishments.

   ☐   I represent my employees' opinions at management meetings.

2. What other actions do you take to provide informal positive feedback?

_____

_____

_____

_____

3. What else could you do?

_____

_____

_____

_____

5

Step 3: Involve Employees in Problem Solving

When a problem arises in the workplace, traditional leaders believe they need to fix the problem. Participative leaders understand they must facilitate the problem-solving process. There is a big difference between these two approaches, and the impact on employee motivation is significant.

Consider the message that the traditional approach sends to employees. When leaders fix problems themselves, employees may perceive that management does not trust them to do the right thing, that management does not have confidence in their ability to solve problems, or that management doesn't think problem solving is part of an employee's role. Whatever the perception, the effect on motivation is negative.

Employees will not be motivated to take risks necessary for innovation if they do not feel trusted, employees will not be motivated to give their best efforts if their talents are not respected, and employees will not be motivated to solve day-to-day problems if no one expects them to do so.

◼ Tap Employee Problem Solvers

Describe any issue or low performance area in your work group that you would like to see changed (employee morale, safety incidents, excessive absenteeism, budget overruns, poor connections with other departments). Identify employees who have the most at stake and the most to contribute to the problem-solving process. Determine when you will obtain their input.

Problem: _____

_____

_____

_____

Employees suited to solve problem: _____

_____

_____

Date to conduct problem-solving session: _____

Step 4: Reward Employee Achievement

Just as the reasons for performing well may seem obvious to leaders, the rewards for achievement may also seem obvious. As a leader, you can probably identify several employee benefits of outstanding achievement immediately (peer recognition, promotion possibility, merit pay increase, self-satisfaction). But would your employees agree with your list? The rewards for achievement in your work group may not be as clear as you think. Also, the rewards may not be as meaningful to employees as you hope.

Remember the expectancy theory of motivation? People are motivated to perform better when they believe they will succeed and that success will be rewarded in a meaningful way. The tricky part for leaders is identifying what is meaningful to other people and then convincing them that those rewards are, in fact, likely. Participative leaders use two strategies to accomplish this.

Involve Employees in Developing Rewards and Recognition.
Although many leaders have little say in how dollars are distributed, they
often have discretion over recognition programs, promotions, and special
rewards. They can also influence company policies. Focus on whatever
areas of influence you have and involve your employees in determining
appropriate rewards.

For instance, if your group is working very hard to complete a special
project on time, don't assume that a beer and pizza party is the only way to
recognize the group's efforts. Given the chance to decide, work groups
may opt for donating to charity in their name, buying a new coffee pot for
the employee lounge, purchasing team T-shirts, or bringing in a motiva-
tional speaker for the next staff meeting. The expenditure is the same, but
the return on investment is much higher when you find out what is meaningful to employees.

One group might decide that if it reaches certain quarterly goals,
employees will get a birthday holiday. Another group might decide that if it
cuts overtime by a specified amount, management will pay for two days of
computer training that the group wants. Still another group might support
a star team program in which one team is recognized each quarter for special contributions.

If you don't know what means the most to your workers, you may invest
in rewards that are not meaningful and therefore are not at all motivating.
How informed are you about what is meaningful to your work group?

Creating High-Value Rewards

First, customize the list below by eliminating any rewards you know are
inappropriate and adding any you think could work. Then rank order the
items from most valued (1) to least valued (10). When you have completed
your own ranking, post the unranked list at a staff meeting and ask
employees to individually rank order the list. Collect the rankings, com-
pute a group ranking, and post the list for your group.

Rank	Possible Employee Recognition / Rewards
_____	Outstanding performer of the month.
_____	Group seminar of employees' choice.
_____	Chance to have lunch with company president.
_____	Write-up in company newspaper.
_____	Pizza party.
_____	Free coffee for a month.
_____	Recognition letter in personnel file.
_____	Department family day (kids come to work).
_____	Other: _____
_____	Other: _____

Influence Company Reward Systems.   Another critical way that leaders can help enhance employee motivation is by influencing company reward systems. If employees feel that achievement is not recognized through formal appraisal and compensation systems, they may not be motivated by department rewards. Keep your ear to the ground, listen for feedback on corporate programs, and represent your employees' thoughts to senior management. It is certainly a challenge to bring reward systems into alignment with performance expectations, but your investment of time will pay off handsomely.

As a participative leader, you can motivate your employees by increasing their involvement in the operations of your group. Focus on developing shared goals, involving everyone in problem solving, providing feedback on performance, and making rewards meaningful.

Chapter 5 Checkpoints

✓ Employee involvement is important to the success of any work group because it increases self-motivation.

✓ Factors that influence employee motivation include mutually developed goals, feedback on performance, joint problem solving, and achievement rewards.

✓ Employees put far more effort into goals if they share in their development and agree that they are attainable.

✓ Participative leaders ensure that important performance goals are measured and that employees obtain performance feedback.

✓ When leaders involve employees in problem solving, everyone wins; more talent is tapped, and employees are recognized for their expertise.

✓ Participative leaders strengthen the power of rewards by identifying what employees consider meaningful and influencing company reward systems.

6 | Employee Empowerment

> **This chapter will help you to:**
>
> - Understand why employee empowerment affects performance.
> - Recognize factors associated with high performance.
> - Learn how to empower employees for high performance.

Doug Lee, supervisor of employee development at a Philadelphia teaching hospital, was asked to put together a new training program on cultural diversity. The program would be introduced at the senior management conference in Baltimore in just four months. Doug knew that the timeline was ambitious, but he also thought it was possible. He contacted content experts and video production people, and he assigned three of his staff to the project full time. He reviewed the course objectives with his manager and clarified audience expectations.

The project was moving along well when Doug's manager told him that the course deadline had changed; the pilot program would have to be presented at the New Orleans conference six weeks earlier than the Baltimore conference. That was just four weeks away.

Doug's first thought was, "No way. We can't possibly be ready." But after further thought, he decided he could meet the new deadline if he could pay his staff overtime. His manager said that would be impossible since there was no extra money in the budget. "Okay, how about comp time? Will you authorize 30 hours of comp time for my three key staff?" Again the answer was negative. Comp time was against policy.

Doug walked away frustrated, mumbling something about the company tying his hands. His manager wondered what he meant. ■

What Do You Think?

Put yourself in Doug's shoes. Then, try to recall a similar situation in your own life.

1. What do you think Doug meant by saying that the company was tying his hands?

    _____
    _____
    _____
    _____
    _____

2. Have you ever been in a situation similar to Doug's? Briefly describe it.

    _____
    _____
    _____
    _____
    _____

3. What three words would best describe your feelings in that situation?

    _____   _____   _____

4. Were you able to perform at your best?   Y   N

5. What would have enabled you to do a better job?

_____

_____

_____

_____

_____

If you are like most supervisors, you were able to remember when someone not only changed the due date for a project you were completing but then failed to provide you with the tools you needed to do the best possible job. And by failing to do so, that manager lost important benefits related to employee empowerment.

BENEFITS OF EMPOWERING EMPLOYEES

6

When leaders empower employees to do their best work, the rewards are obvious. Customer satisfaction, product quality, and the work climate all improve. Empowered employees do a better job because they feel more responsible for end results. They also assume greater ownership for continuous process improvement when they are given the authority to try new methods and the tools to learn new processes. Because expectations are clear, talent is utilized, and success is likely. Morale is generally high in empowered workplaces, and stress is low. Any stress associated with the excitement and hard work tends to be motivating rather than debilitating. High morale and low stress reduce absenteeism and employee turnover.

FACTORS RELATED TO HIGH PERFORMANCE

If you were to ask your employees what they need to do their best work, what do you think they would say? Training? Equipment? More time? Whatever their answers, you probably would hear reference to three factors associated with high-performance work groups: direction, authority, and resources. A look at these factors will illustrate why your ability to empower employees is so important to high productivity.

6

Clear Direction

For employees to produce desired results, they need to direct and redirect their energy toward clear targets. During any given day, employees are faced with numerous decisions related to priorities. They may have to decide whether it is better to be on time with a shipment or to delay shipment until the order is complete, whether it is more important to satisfy a customer or contain costs on a project, or whether it is more advisable to risk losing a job by not agreeing to an unreasonable completion date or risk disappointing a customer by not meeting the promised completion date.

When employees understand performance expectations they know where to direct their energies in order to perform at their best. Otherwise, they are basically shooting in the dark and hoping to hit a bull's-eye.

Shared Authority and Accountability

In high-performance work groups, both authority and responsibility are shared through appropriate delegation. To achieve outstanding results, employees must influence decisions related to tasks and share accountability for success or failure. Participative leaders provide general direction rather than detailed how-to instructions. Allowing employees to influence how something is accomplished builds confidence and develops personal commitment. Similarly, if employees are recognized for success or asked to explain failures, they will feel more accountable for results. Accountability is necessary for outstanding performance.

Necessary Resources

To do a quality job, employees need resources. They need talent, equipment, training, and tools, and they need prompt access to such resources. No amount of direction or delegation can make up for a lack of resources.

You might assume that because this factor seems obvious, most supervisors would provide the required resources. However, while many supervisors do think of equipment, most do not adequately consider the talent, tools, and training needs of their work group. Because each resource influences performance in a different way, leaders should pay attention to all resources.

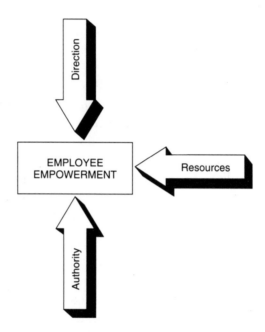

THREE STEPS TO EMPOWERING EMPLOYEES

Participative leaders empower employees by influencing the three factors associated with high performance: direction, authority, and resources. If you want to influence those factors and increase empowerment in your work group, concentrate on these leadership actions: communicate, delegate, and support.

Step 1: Communicate

How well do you communicate performance-related information? To help employees perform their best, you need to clarify expectations, discuss priorities, and provide interim results. The time you invest in clear communication will make a noticeable difference in your group's performance.

Clarify Expectations. Although it may seem simple, explaining what you expect from others is not always easy. First, you must decide what it is that you actually want, and then you must communicate those expectations to your employees.

To determine what you want from your work group, try to imagine what a successful week, a successful quarter, or a successful year would look like. What would be good indicators that your work group is meeting your expectations for a high-performance group? You might consider productivity numbers, budget variance, overtime, grievances, on-time deliveries, quality indicators, customer feedback, number of new ideas, attendance at meetings, volunteers for shift work, or new skills acquired. Also consider how you expect people in your work group to treat one another.

■ Measuring Performance Expectations

List any performance indicators that are appropriate for your work group. For each measure describe a target standard, such as "94 percent satisfactory," "not more than two remakes per quarter," or simply "generally agreed to be good."

Measure	Standard
1. _____	_____
2. _____	_____
3. _____	_____
4. _____	_____
5. _____	_____

Discuss Priorities. Once you have clearly identified and communicated your expectations, pay attention to priorities because it is here that employees sometimes have difficulty in meeting the needs of their leaders. Perhaps in the first quarter of the fiscal year, service to customers was so important that you wanted employees to log overtime and incur even unusual costs to satisfy major clients. However, in the second quarter of the year, you might be under so much fire to contain costs that you expect employees to be polite but not to grant any unusual requests. How are your employees to know? They won't know unless you regularly discuss important priorities. If you do so, you will avoid many disappointments and encourage more of the behavior that is likely to meet your expectations.

■ Work Group Priorities

Respond to the following statements and questions. Then share your answers with your work group.

1. List three to six performance priorities for your group (quality, quantity).

6

   _____   _____

   _____   _____

   _____   _____

2. List any service priorities (courtesy, timeliness, customization).

   _____

   _____

   _____

3. List any budget priorities (waste, overtime).

   _____

   _____

   _____

4. List three teamwork behaviors you would like to see in your group.

   _____

   _____

   _____

5. Do any of these priorities conflict? If so, which should take precedence?

_____

_____

_____

_____

Provide Interim Results.   Once you have communicated your expectations and clarified priorities, you need to provide data on interim results so employees can assess to what degree their efforts are resulting in success. Even negative results are informational and better than no performance data. The only logical reason for changing work processes or modifying behavior is to produce better results. If we don't know how we are doing in the short term, we are unlikely to invest much energy in improvement.

Communicate interim results related to the corporate and department priorities you have been emphasizing. For instance, if you have established internal customer service as a priority, don't wait for the annual survey results. Share the results of quarterly feedback surveys from other departments, post all internal customer feedback letters each week, or invite a panel of internal customers in once a month to discuss their perceptions of your department's service.

If innovation is a top priority, consider distributing a "Great Ideas" sheet each month that describes the idea, recognizes the individual or group that generated the idea, and illustrates how the idea will be used. Or you might construct a lightbulb barometer poster as a visual reminder of the quantity of ideas generated each week. Whatever your performance priorities, be certain to measure interim progress and then communicate that progress to your work group.

Step 2: Delegate

Effective delegation is arguably the most difficult leadership action related to employee empowerment. It is difficult because it requires both a shift in leadership thinking and specific implementation skills. The shift in thinking involves long-term versus short-term benefits. The implementation skills include clarifying limits of authority, agreeing on measures of success, coaching on the job, and sharing any glory.

Shift to a Long-Term Focus.   One of the biggest obstacles to effective delegation is short-term thinking. Leaders who do not delegate well often complain that delegation takes too much time, that it's easier to do the task themselves, and that employees won't do as good a job. Have any of these thoughts crossed your mind, or do you have additional reasons why it's not worthwhile to delegate more to the people in your work group?

■ Why Don't You Delegate More?

Check off each reason that has stopped you from delegating in your work group. Add any other reasons that come to mind.

- ☐ It's easier to do most things myself.
- ☐ Employees can't do most things as well as I can.
- ☐ I don't have time to teach someone how to do my job.
- ☐ People in my work group don't want any more responsibility.
- ☐ I will become less valuable to the company if I delegate more.
- ☐ The more I delegate, the more policing I will have to do.
- ☐ _____
- ☐ _____

Rest assured that the beliefs you checked off are held by a large number of supervisors. They are common thoughts that are grounded in a short-term reward paradigm. Each statement has a grain of truth in it if you consider only the short term. Initially, delegating does take more time and effort than doing a task yourself. Employees may not embrace a new responsibility immediately, and you may feel less valuable as you begin to reshape your contribution to the company. When you first begin to delegate, you will have to monitor progress more, and you will probably have to coach a few individuals.

However, when you shift to a long-term mindset, the rewards of delegating become far more obvious. Employees who are encouraged to accept new responsibilities develop more confidence in themselves, and stretch their own limits. The employee who is coached on a task today can coach a co-worker next month, freeing you to focus on other responsibilities. While early monitoring is often critical to successful delegation, in the long term employees who have responsibility for a task or project will monitor performance themselves, reducing the amount of supervisory policing necessary.

A supervisor who develops people and facilitates department progress toward organizational goals is far more valuable than one who focuses only on completing tasks. Shifting to a long-term mentality will not enhance only employee empowerment but will also enhance your career.

Clarify Boundaries of Authority.   Once you have adjusted your mindset, the first implementation skill necessary for effective delegation is clarifying the boundaries of authority related to any task. For instance, which decisions will you make and which would you like your employees to make? Who will contact customers and senior management regarding the task or project? Who will have budgeting or requisition authority?

The basic message you need to communicate as a leader is when you want to be involved. If you and the person to whom you are delegating are clear about boundaries in the beginning, you will avoid confusion and conflict later.

▮ What Limits Do You Generally Prefer?

To identify any limits that you should communicate when delegating a task to someone in your work group, complete this unfinished sentence: "I generally prefer that employees check with me before they . . ."

1. _____

2. _____

3. _____

4. _____

5. _____

The next time you delegate a task or project, communicate those general limits as well as any limits that are unique to the particular task.

Agree on Measures of Success.   If you and the employees you supervise agree on measures of success, you will make your work life much easier and increase the probability of successful delegation. Depending on the type of task or project, the measures you agree on can be quite formal (a customer feedback report, written evaluations to a program presentation, 50 percent reduction in safety violations) or rather informal ("to the satisfaction of our work group." "an observable change in co-worker cooperation"). The more specific the measure, the lower the probability of any disagreement regarding performance success.

Regardless of the type of measure, a leader should make certain that minimal success conditions are clear. What is to be completed, by when, and to what degree must be *explicitly* clear. Have you ever been asked to complete an assignment, agreed, and then had someone annoyed when you had not completed it in a week? Or perhaps you were asked to research something by a certain date. You did, but when you shared the information, the delegator did not find your research complete. Perhaps you were asked to go back and spend more time on the job. In both cases, the delegation was not effective because the specifics of what constituted success were not agreed upon in the beginning. Expectations were unclear.

Coach, Rather Than Do.   For delegation to be an effective means of employee empowerment, leaders must be realistic about coaching individuals new to a process or task. It is unrealistic to assume that because you turn over a task you will be totally removed from the project immediately. Your employees may need some coaching in the early stages of acquiring a new responsibility.

What they don't need is someone to do the job for them out of frustration. Leave responsibility where you have newly placed it and provide coaching as requested. Use thought-provoking questions (What do you think is most important to the customer?) rather than directives (Give them the delivery, but not the price) or sermons (Now, you know we've discussed time and again how important delivery time is to that customer). Be available when you're needed, but don't be afraid to demonstrate confidence by encouraging employees to find their own answers. Remember, good coaches always inspire and often teach, but they never do the job for their players.

Share the Glory.   If you want delegation to be a successful tool for enhancing employee empowerment, be sure that you share the recognition when someone performs admirably. Nothing is more demoralizing than to work hard, achieve a level of success, and watch from the wings while someone else takes the bows. Leaders who want to use delegation effectively need to be very aggressive about directing recognition to the deserving party.

Step 3: Support

Empowered employees also need support in the form of equipment, training, talent, and tools. You can communicate what you expect, delegate authority appropriately, and still not see the results you want if your work group does not have the resources to do the job.

When considering what tasks you would like your work group to handle (scheduling, inventory control, customer contact), also consider what skills they need to do that job well. For instance, if you want to delegate more budgeting to a work group, assess what the group knows about budgeting in general and the budget process within your firm, specifically. The group might need a course, printed guidelines, or on-the-job coaching.

If you want employees to assume responsibility for customer contact, they may need training in listening or interviewing skills. They will certainly need release time to build relationships and gather customer feedback.

■ Work Group Support

Check off any support you can provide for your work group. Then, ask your employees what they think and prioritize the list.

Equipment
- ☐ Computers.
- ☐ Software.
- ☐ _____
- ☐ _____

Training
- ☐ Group decision making.
- ☐ Quality measurement tools.
- ☐ _____
- ☐ _____

Talent
- ☐ Additional full-time help.
- ☐ Temporary process leadership.
- ☐ _____
- ☐ _____

Tools
- ☐ Guidelines.
- ☐ Measurements.
- ☐ Performance feedback.
- ☐ _____
- ☐ _____

6

Chapter 6 Checkpoints

✓ Employee empowerment leads to high performance.

✓ To empower employees, leaders need to communicate, delegate, and support.

✓ Participative leaders communicate expectations, priorities, and interim results.

✓ To delegate effectively, leaders need to:
  - Shift to a long-term focus.
  - Clarify boundaries of authority.
  - Agree on measures of success.
  - Coach appropriately.
  - Share recognition.

✓ Employee empowerment requires support for excellent performance, including equipment, training, talent, and tools.

7 | Facilitating Teamwork

This chapter will help you to:

- Understand why teamwork is important.
- Recognize factors associated with teamwork.
- Learn how to facilitate teamwork in your group.

Cynthia Jones, head teller in a branch office of a major San Francisco bank, recently supervised conversion of teller terminals to an on-line system that allows immediate access to customer records. When the conversion was complete, Cynthia realized that other systems changes were likely, and she wanted to see more cooperation during the next conversion. She didn't want to see older and younger tellers competing to see who could learn the new system faster. Neither did she want to see some tellers resisting training with other tellers because they were "too negative."

In the next conversion, she hoped that tellers might help one another practice and celebrate as each teller passed the competency test. Cindy was certain that better teamwork would make future conversions go more smoothly, but she wasn't sure what she could do differently to promote such teamwork. ■

■ **What Do You Think?**

Based on your own experience with work changes over the years, what do you think Cindy should do to facilitate more teamwork in her group?

_____

_____

_____

_____

_____

If your advice to Cindy included identifying benefits to tellers for cooperating, developing processes that encourage cooperation, and being a good role model herself, you are on the right track. All of these are important if a leader is to facilitate teamwork within a work group. But before we explore each of these areas, let's identify why a leader would want to invest the time and energy in developing a cohesive team of workers.

7

THE BENEFITS OF TEAMWORK

When work groups develop synergy—a cohesiveness that significantly enhances the group's power—many benefits are apparent. Perhaps most important in today's fast-paced, competitive marketplace are increased responsiveness and creativity. Work groups that develop teamwork respond to change rapidly because they understand each other's jobs, trust each other, and want to see the whole team succeed. Synergistic work groups are also more innovative, because they have learned to tap the full potential of all employees, opening a wide range of ideas, skills, and talents. The open atmosphere allows risk taking, which is necessary for innovation.

Another benefit of increased teamwork is a more positive work climate. As trust, communication, and cooperation increase, stress decreases. Spontaneous celebrations, humor, and genuine caring are more common, and people seem to enjoy their work. A solid team makes life much easier for a supervisor.

■ Benefits of Teamwork

Check off any benefits that are important to you. Add your own ideas.

- ☐ More pitching in.
- ☐ Less gossip.
- ☐ More positive energy.
- ☐ Less individual competition.
- ☐ Better employee conflict management.
- ☐ Less refereeing by supervisor.
- ☐ More flexibility in job assignments.
- ☐ Less territorialism.
- ☐ More fun.
- ☐ More ideas.
- ☐ More involvement.
- ☐ _____
- ☐ _____

7

FACTORS ASSOCIATED WITH TEAMWORK

Groups that work together effectively usually recognize the rewards of working as a team. They know what a good team looks like, and they focus on their team process as well as on their tasks.

Rewards of Teamwork

It takes time and effort to become a cohesive work team. People have to get to know one another, develop trust, create shared goals, balance contributions, manage conflict, and make decisions by consensus. All of these behaviors require discipline and learning. In many cases, they also require breaking old habits and shifting mindsets. Any discomfort associated with personal change must be offset by substantial rewards if we expect people to change their behavior. The first question you should ask yourself as a leader is, "What is in it for my employees if they work together as a team?"

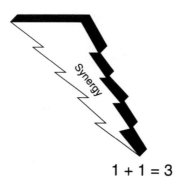

$$1 + 1 = 3$$

Synergy is one benefit of teamwork.

A Model of Effective Teamwork

Members of a work group need a clear model of how an effective work team functions. A work group might be motivated to work better together, but still not understand *how* to work better together. If a group has a model of behaviors that lead to better teamwork, it will be able to assess its own strengths and weaknesses against the model and direct its energy toward improving any shortcomings.

Focus on Team Process

Effective teamwork requires regular maintenance. Team members need to focus on their own communication, conflict management, and cooperation levels as well as on problem-solving and decision-making skills. They need to regularly revisit their shared purpose and joint goals, and share in each other's successes. If the focus is solely on *what* is produced rather than on *how* it is produced, the team will not reach its potential.

THREE STEPS TO FACILITATING TEAMWORK

Participative leaders can facilitate teamwork by making teamwork rewarding, providing a model of effective teams, and encouraging a focus on team process. While each of these actions requires some effort, you will probably find the rewards well worth your investment.

Step 1: Make Teamwork Rewarding

Leaders can increase the attention paid to teamwork by developing rewards for effective teamwork. Such rewards might involve performance reviews, recognition programs, and enjoyable team meetings. Let's look at how leaders can influence each of these areas.

Include Teamwork in Performance Reviews.   Although many leaders today are asked to foster teamwork within their work groups, most corporations have a long way to go in developing appraisal and compensation systems that reinforce teamwork. If that is the case in your company, you will have to be particularly inventive in incorporating teamwork into your performance reviews.

First, try to get a few items formally added to your organization's appraisal form. Meanwhile, in your own meetings with employees, emphasize the importance of behaviors that are associated with teamwork (effective communications, willingness to help, openness to the ideas of others). Discuss how teamwork positively affects your work group and how a lack of teamwork negatively affects the group. To discuss these two elements, you must be clear yourself. What is the impact of teamwork on your group?

How Does Teamwork Affect Your Group?

1. Describe how your group benefits when employees cooperate as a team. Consider the positive impact on quality, customer service, the work climate, and individuals in your work group.

   _____

   _____

   _____

   _____

   _____

2. Describe how your group is negatively affected when individuals put their own needs and comfort ahead of what is best for the group.

   _____

   _____

   _____

   _____

   _____

Develop Team Recognition Programs.   Another reward of teamwork should be recognition for cooperating as part of a group. Unfortunately, many companies recognize only individual performers, thereby encouraging competition and hoarding of ideas. If teamwork is a priority for your group, you will need to creatively recognize employee behaviors that focus on the good of the group, rather than on the good of the individual, and on joint efforts, rather than on stellar performances.

For instance, if your group works a different shift, helps with tasks outside its normal domain, or resolves a problem rapidly, you could hold a pizza party for the team, write complimentary letters for personnel folders, send congratulatory fruit baskets to each member's family, or simply provide free juice and coffee for a week. You could decorate their work area with balloons and banners or have a trophy case made up and fill it with team trophies over the years. A simple note from you or a brief thank-you talk might also be meaningful.

Consider the likes and dislikes of your work group to determine which recognition ideas will mean the most to them. Remember, a reward is a reward only if the recipients consider it one.

■ Your Work Group

List recognition ideas that you think your whole work group would appreciate. Include some ideas that do not require any funding. Later, ask your work group what they think.

_____   _____
_____   _____
_____   _____
_____   _____
_____   _____
_____   _____

Make Team Meetings Enjoyable.   Another reward for being on a team is attending enjoyable meetings. If meetings are dull or, at worst, combative, people will not think working as a team is much fun. You can make meetings more enjoyable by encouraging five minutes for socializing at the beginning or end of each meeting or by starting each meeting off with an ice breaker (team trivia, baby picture match, sharing successes of the week, discussing which priorities are hot).

You can also rotate leadership of the meeting by having different members of your group facilitate each week. Invite guest speakers (senior management, human resources, visiting dignitaries) to speak for the first 15 minutes of a meeting. Occasionally, hold off-site dinner or lunch meetings, show a videotape, or pass around work-related cartoons. Don't be afraid to share a joke or two.

7

■ What Are Your Group's Meetings Like?

Check off any responses that apply to your meetings. Then, ask your work group to do the same. Discuss how to improve any shortcomings that surface.

Our work group meetings . . .

☐ are pretty interesting.	☐ are usually dull.
☐ generally start on time.	☐ are usually late starting.
☐ usually end on time.	☐ generally run overtime.
☐ include humor.	☐ are usually serious.
☐ help us get to know one another.	☐ focus only on tasks.
☐ are held in good locations.	☐ are held in bad locations.
☐ are productive.	☐ are a waste of time.
☐ _____	☐ _____
☐ _____	☐ _____

Step 2: Provide a Model of Effective Teamwork

Leaders can also facilitate effective teamwork by providing a model for employees to use in judging the appropriateness of their behaviors. Leaders can do this by offering training that outlines characteristics of effective teams (commitment, contribution, communication, cooperation, conflict management, change management, and connections) and describes behaviors that enhance those characteristics. Leaders can also provide examples of effective teams for workers to emulate. The most powerful leadership approach provides both a model and practical examples for benchmarking.

Teach Behaviors of Effective Teams.   You have several options available for teaching behaviors of effective teams. You can bring in a team specialist (internal or external) to conduct a training program, you can take such training yourself and then teach your group, or you can read any of the many books about effective work teams and develop your own model for your group.

Each option requires a different level of investment and expertise. If you have a corporate trainer available, you will have to pay little and spend little preparation time yourself. If you bring in an outside trainer, you will not have to invest much time yourself, but you will have to invest some of your budget. If you decide to read a book and develop your model yourself, you will have to invest very little money, but you will need to invest a good deal of your time.

Weigh each option and decide which approach is best for your group but do provide a model so that everyone sees the same behaviors that contribute to effective teamwork.

■ Which Training Approach?

Check yes or no in response to each statement. When you have completed the activity you will have a better idea of which method is best for you.

7

( ) Yes   ( ) No   Good corporate team trainers are available.

( ) Yes   ( ) No   I have a budget for outside trainers.

( ) Yes   ( ) No   An outside trainer would be better for my group.

( ) Yes   ( ) No   I would like to read a book about effective teams.

( ) Yes   ( ) No   I have the time to develop training based on a book.

( ) Yes   ( ) No   My group pays more attention to internal trainers.

( ) Yes   ( ) No   My group pays more attention to external trainers.

( ) Yes   ( ) No   My group pays more attention to me as a trainer.

Provide Benchmarking Examples of Teams.   Another powerful way to teach your work group about effective teamwork is to introduce them to high-performance teams. These teams might be within your division, within your company, or in another company—not necessarily in the same industry. The important criterion is that the model team is accessible to your group for benchmarking by visitation, video conference, or videotape.

The most ideal arrangement is for you to invite the model group to make a presentation to your group to discuss its success factors. The presentation would then be followed by a site visit for observation and interaction with the whole team. Afterward, members of your group could discuss which of the factors outlined are most important to your team, how each factor could be assessed, and how each factor could be improved. You could reinforce such visitations with video training programs, seminar speakers, or independent study groups.

■ Effective Work Teams

List any effective work teams within your geographical area.

Within Your Company

_____

_____

Suppliers

_____

_____

Friendly Competitors

_____

_____

Step 3: Encourage a Focus on Team Process

Once teams develop an understanding of effective teamwork, they need to regularly compare their work group's behaviors to behaviors associated with the appropriate model. It is not enough to learn how a work group *should* be functioning; it is essential to continuously improve how it *is* functioning. Leaders can encourage a focus on team process by helping teams assess their present functioning and enhance their future functioning.

Assess Present Work Group Functioning.   As a leader, you can help your work group assess its present functioning. Perhaps most important, you can convey the message that group process is as important as group product. In fact, it may be more important because the process continues long after a particular product has been shipped.

Processes that work groups use to make decisions, manage conflict, set goals, measure results, and adapt to change all affect the quality and quantity of their product as well as the quality of people attracted to their work unit. A leader's opinion of the value of process will strongly affect a group, and a leader conveys an opinion more strongly with actions than with words.

If you say process is important, but you never allow time for your work group to focus on its process, your group will assume that process is not that important. If you encourage process assessment, but you won't allow employees any time to improve, your group will also assume process is not important. As a leader, you need to walk your talk about process.

7

■ The Importance of Process

List any actions you can take immediately to convey the message that your work group's process is important (discuss at a meeting, write a memo, circulate an article, bring in a guest speaker).

_____

_____

_____

_____

In addition, you can support assessment of group process by providing employees with inventories, customer feedback, and your own observations of the group's functioning. If you have observed that your group does not seem to communicate well, you might share that feedback and ask members to list behaviors they consider important to effective communication (listening to others' ideas, not taking disagreement personally, stating problems as questions rather than complaints). Group members should then rate themselves on each of the behaviors on the compiled list. You could suggest that the group reevaluate its communication skills in six months to see if any progress has been made.

■ Resources

List any resources within the categories below that might help you secure surveys, inventories, or profiles to use in evaluating group process.

Other supervisors: _____

_____

Human resources: _____

_____

An outside consultant: _____

_____

A book or journal: _____

_____

A quality/management association: _____

_____

Support Process Improvement.   Leaders should also be certain that work groups move on to process improvement. You can demonstrate support for improvement by sanctioning use of time for process improvement and by providing training in problem-solving techniques. Encourage your work group to target areas for improvement on a regular (monthly or quarterly) basis. Perhaps you could devote one department meeting a month exclusively to group process issues. You could encourage subgroup task forces to address improvement areas. Or you could develop a suggestion system for improving a particular process area.

Employees need skills as well as time if they are to improve their group functioning. Leaders can support such development by providing training in problem-solving techniques such as brainstorming, multivoting, root cause analysis, or consensus decision making. You can view video training programs together at staff meetings. Or you can send representatives for training with the understanding that they will return and teach the rest of your work group what they learned. You can also bring in a training program to your department. Whatever the method, training in process improvement techniques is one way that leaders can facilitate effective teamwork.

7

Chapter 7 Checkpoints

✓ Participative leaders facilitate effective teamwork.

✓ Factors associated with effective teamwork include rewards for teamwork, a clear model of effective teamwork, and a focus on team process.

✓ Leaders can make teamwork rewarding by including teamwork in performance reviews, developing team recognition programs, and making team meetings enjoyable.

✓ Leaders can provide a model of effective teamwork by teaching characteristics of effective teams and providing benchmarking opportunities with effective teams.

✓ Participative leaders encourage a focus on team process by helping employees assess and improve group functioning and by supporting improvement efforts.

Post-Test

Assess your understanding of participative leadership by answering the following questions.

1. Participative leadership came about because of a need for more employee _____.

2. Participative leaders are more like _____, than bosses.

3. Participative leaders focus on enhancing commitment, motivation, performance, and _____.

4. A clear _____ of success makes sure that everyone in a work group is working toward the same end results.

5. One way that leaders can motive employees is to _____ them in decisions that affect their work.

6. To empower employees, participative leaders _____ tasks effectively.

7. Participative leaders _____ teamwork to create synergy within their work group.

8. Leaders should support employees by providing resources such as time, talent, training, and _____.

9. Leaders can use performance feedback to motivate and _____ employee energy.

10. Four actions that participative leaders can take are to: inspire, involve, _____, and facilitate.

Business Skills Express Series

This growing series of books addresses a broad range of key business skills and topics to meet the needs of employees, human resource departments, and training consultants.

To obtain information about these and other Business Skills Express books, please call Irwin Professional Publishing toll free at: 1-800-634-3966.

Effective Performance Management
ISBN   1-55623-867-3

Hiring the Best
ISBN   1-55623-865-7

Writing that Works
ISBN   1-55623-856-8

Customer Service Excellence
ISBN   1-55623-969-6

Writing for Business Results
ISBN   1-55623-854-1

Powerful Presentation Skills
ISBN   1-55623-870-3

Meetings that Work
ISBN   1-55623-866-5

Effective Teamwork
ISBN   1-55623-880-0

Time Management
ISBN   1-55623-888-6

Assertiveness Skills
ISBN   1-55623-857-6

Motivation at Work
ISBN   1-55623-868-1

Overcoming Anxiety at Work
ISBN   1-55623-869-X

Positive Politics at Work
ISBN   1-55623-879-7

Telephone Skills at Work
ISBN   1-55623-858-4

Managing Conflict at Work
ISBN   1-55623-890-8

The New Supervisor: Skills for Success
ISBN   1-55623-762-6

The *Americans with Disabilities Act:* What Supervisors Need to Know
ISBN   1-55623-889-4

Managing the Demands of Work and Home
ISBN   0-7863-0221-6

Effective Listening Skills
ISBN   0-7863-0102-4

Goal Management at Work
ISBN   0-7863-0225-9

Positive Attitudes at Work
ISBN   0-7863-0100-8

Supervising the Difficult Employee
ISBN   0-7863-0219-4

Cultural Diversity in the Workplace
ISBN   0-7863-0125-2

Managing Change in the Workplace
ISBN   0-7863-0162-7

Negotiating for Business Results
ISBN   0-7863-0114-7

Practical Business Communication
ISBN   0-7863-0227-5

High Performance Speaking
ISBN   0-7863-0222-4

Delegation Skills
ISBN   0-7863-0105-9

Coaching Skills: A Guide for Supervisors
ISBN   0-7863-0220-8

Customer Service and the Telephone
ISBN   0-7863-0224-0

Creativity at Work
ISBN   0-7863-0223-2

Effective Interpersonal Relationships
ISBN   0-7863-0255-0

The Participative Leader
ISBN   0-7863-0252-6

Building Customer Loyalty
ISBN   0-7863-0253-4

Getting and Staying Organized
ISBN   0-7863-0254-2

Total Quality Selling
ISBN   0-7863-0324-7

Business Etiquette
ISBN   0-7863-0323-9

Empowering Employees
ISBN   0-7863-0314-X

Training Skills for Supervisors
ISBN   0-7863-0313-1

Moving Meetings
ISBN   0-7863-0333-6

Multicultural Customer Service
ISBN   0-7863-0332-8